ENDORSEMENTS

"This book is like its author-kind, loving and empathic—it's a must read for anyone seeking a higher form of love."

—Michael Parker, Programmer, Awtec

"I recommend The Agape Book for anyone interested in learning about the mystery of what we call Love."

—Richelle C. Lester, Law Office of Richelle C. Lester, PLLC, Attorney at Law.

"This book is a wonderful collection of many profound levels of love so eloquently defined."

—Beatrice Rose, Retired

"KC Love has written a must-read for anyone interested in learning the depths of Agape love. Agape teaches others how the smallest act of kindness can change a life. Read this book!!"

—Mallory Beard, President, Beard & Associates LLC

agape

KC LOVE

Copyright © 2024 KC Love

All rights reserved. No part of this publication in print or in electronic format may be reproduced, stored in a retrieval system, or transmitted in any form or by any means, electronic, mechanical, photocopying, recording, or otherwise without the prior written permission of the publisher.

The scanning, uploading, and distribution of this book without permission is a theft of the author's intellectual property. Thank you for your support of the author's rights.

Editing, design, and distribution by Bublish

978-1-647047-00-9 (eBook)
978-1-647047-01-6 (paperback)
978-1-647047-02-3 (hardcover)

Contents

Introduction vii

PART 1
Foundations of Love

Chapter 1   The Strength of Love 3
Chapter 2   The Ethics of Agape 8
Chapter 3   American Life 12
Chapter 4   Practicing Love in Everyday Life 17

PART 2
What Happens to People When They Are Deprived of Love

Chapter 5   The Profound Impacts of Lacking Love 25

PART 3
How We Can Improve Our Lives and the Lives of Others by Being More Loving

Chapter 6   Love as a Teacher 31

Conclusion 37
Bonus Chapter: Early Scholarship on Love 41
References 45
About the Author 47

Introduction

Agape is a Greek word meaning *love*. There are numerous ways to describe this love, but in the Christian tradition, it is known as *agape*, or the love of God for humanity. In modern life, we can think of agape as a broader love—the love for humanity itself and the love for everyone facing the one thing we all have in common: the struggle of living.

People are born with the ability to love, but throughout our lives, when we suffer loss, abuse, and hardship, that love is tested. As we grow older, it's easy to lose pieces of ourselves we wish we could get back. *Agape* can allow us to find those pieces again so we can rediscover and be true to who we really are. It will not only help us be our best selves but help us find the best in others and focus on the positives rather than the negatives in life. We may not always know how to show more love, but we can remember a way we can practice it by using a simple acronym, LOVE: Let Our Virtue Emerge.

It seems now more than ever, the world around us is lacking agape. Every time we turn on the news, scroll through social media, or even peruse new titles on the shelves of a local bookstore, there's something new to be afraid of, another big catastrophe threatening the world. Strife pervades our environment, almost as if it's in the air. Everyone is locked into an us-versus-them mentality that seems impossible to shake.

The emergence of modern technology has made this mindset more visible to a larger number of people, but it would be short-sighted to suggest it is something new. Our inherent prejudices and proclivity for violence has plagued humankind from the very beginning. Though the internet has granted a platform for people with misdirected anger to vent and volley digital vitriol from person-to-person with alarming ease, it's merely a facilitator of behavior we've demonstrated for ages. We cannot return to some magical time during which people were less animated about their dislike for others, because those expressions of animus have always been present. They are now simply taking new shapes as times change, like some foul chemical concoction flowing to fit a different beaker in an alchemist's lab.

Fortunately, there is a cure for this illness that seems to have infected many of us to some degree or another. The us-versus-them mentality can be overturned by seeking out similarities with people you might oppose. Strip away the politics, the social tensions, and the negative dispositions that have been carefully cultivated over the years, and, if you're honest with yourself, you'll find many more similarities than differences. When you focus on the basic essence of what it means to be human, you'll find someone who is not a stranger, despite the major differences you might have.

Both love and hate are natural parts of the human psyche, and whichever we choose to nurture will become stronger. Though we may not be able to eradicate hate from our lives entirely, consistently choosing love can, over time, lessen our impulse to respond to negative situations with hate. We must also choose to practice forgiveness, because it and agape are intimately tied. Forgiveness is powered by empathy and understanding the motivations of people who have wronged us. That understanding will help us build a better world, a world in which people who have taken wrong turns in their lives feel able to make amends instead of being trapped in a life in which they make things worse for others. Practicing peace and forgiveness will not be a short battle, nor will it be won if founded on negative energy.

Committing to LOVE is hard work. It means asking every day, "How can I show more agape in my life?" That query will not always be easy to answer, but everyone can find a response that works for them. The world needs more love, and every one of us can contribute in a unique, personal way.

Virtue consists of many excellent qualities, here is a list of synonyms we all can try to incorporate into our lives. Integrity, honesty, goodness, righteousness, honor, ethics, morals, decency, decorum, etiquette, propriety. Imagine if we all walked in virtue and let these synonyms emerge in us how the world would change.

PART 1
Foundations of Love

CHAPTER 1

The Strength of Love

My journey with agape began in 2010, when I made the decision to leave my husband of eighteen years. I realized I needed to reexamine what love meant. Like so many others, the love I'd inherently understood as a child had become harder to hold on to. Sometimes, no matter how much we want to approach the world from a place of love, life wears us down. We may go on autopilot, allowing ourselves to pass our days without concern for others. This practice can lead to less empathy for other people and more anger when they do something, intentionally or unintentionally, to inconvenience or disrespect us. It can cause us to become reactionary and behave in ways that don't align with how we see ourselves, which can lead to even more anger.

As I thought about what love truly means, I came up with the acronym LOVE: Let Our Virtue Emerge. I made it a practice every day to pay attention to situations in which I did not show love and figure out how I could have done better. Over time, it became a habit, and through that habit, I was able to change the way I approached others. I realized even when we let life take away some of our virtue—our sense of right and wrong—learning to LOVE will allow us to take it back.

If you were to ask the average person whether they live a moral life, most people would answer in the affirmative. Healthy adults have a sense of right and wrong founded in lessons learned from parents, friends, spiritual leaders, and anyone else they see as having moral authority. But though many people spend their time practicing ethical behavior and trying to do right by others, the idea of morality may live in the background of their minds, taking a back seat to other motivations and seldom receiving any close inspection.

A key issue we face is the difficulty of defining morality and what it means to live a moral life. It is easy to say you adhere to some principles, but when not everyone shares the same principles, whose interpretation of morality is correct? Does living a moral life translate to simply following the law? Laws change all the time, from state to state and country to country. Something common fifty years ago might not be even remotely legal now. Some people believe living morally simply involves behaving in a stereotypically "good" fashion, such as donating to charity and volunteering time to worthy causes. If that's the case, hundreds of corporations—many of which have questionable motives—are examples of the highest character. But the most common determiner of what is right and what is wrong might be religion, which has inspired some of history's greatest heroes and humblest servants across the world. However, throughout history, from the Spanish Inquisition to modern acts of radical Islamic terrorism, pious people have misread their faith's holy words to justify terrible acts.

If none of these ideals alone accurately define morality, what does? Is morality an action one can take, or is it a philosophical perspective or worldview one must embrace? Is it the embodiment of both? Regardless, I think we can all agree on one thing: to be moral is to approach life with love. Love inspires piety, charity, selflessness, and awe. Love brings people together, crosses the widest of divides, and overcomes deep-seated grievances. It is uniquely human, and people are at their best when they act out of love.

Of course, love comes in different forms that motivate people in a variety of ways, but one of the most important forms of love—especially in times of instability and divisiveness—is love for humanity. Some might term this *kinship*, which is finding common ground with people who come from different backgrounds. Kinship is the ability to see similarity and stake warmth with another person for no other reason than shared humanness.

Countless people have lived their lives full of love and serve as examples of this priceless asset in modern life. Some are household names today, like Gandhi, Mandela, and Tubman. Others are newer and not yet as imprinted in our collective consciousness, like Ellen Johnson Sirleaf and Leymah Gbowee, Liberian peace activists who led thousands of women in a movement for harmony and toward an end to the civil war ravaging their country. Sirleaf and Gbowee were successful largely due to fostering understanding with their political foes rather than demonizing anyone. Despite the horrible damage being inflicted upon the country, they did not give in to the temptation to paint the opposition as evil. The movement these women led focused on shedding religious blinders and knitting together Muslim and Christian women, bringing unity to a traditionally disparate population. Sirleaf and Gbowee encouraged their supporters to follow the path of love and compassion for all humanity. In other words, they believed in the power of agape to heal national wounds and inspire people to be their best selves.

Another modern example is Liu Xiaobo, a human rights activist in China. For decades, Xiaobo was a critic of the Chinese government's domestic policies restricting citizens' rights and the treatment of political protestors who questioned China's ruling class. He rallied his countrymen to numerous causes, including

Chinese recognition of Taiwan as an independent nation and freedom from Chinese rule for Tibet. Xiaobo's criticisms of his government were strong, but his writings always pushed supporters toward the path of nonviolence and even love for their enemies. He believed in the power of love to triumph where fear, hatred, and violence had failed.

After enduring the terrible protests at Tiananmen Square that left many dead, Xiaobo wrote, "That bloody dawn in 1989 . . . taught me to recognize the warmth and inner strength of love, and gave me new appreciation of what is most important in life" (Xiaobo 2012, 292). Xiaobo found love for his persecutors even after they had done so much to hurt him and those he struggled alongside. That love afforded him the strength to endure decades of rebellion against an authoritarian government.

One of the most notable testaments to the influence of agape is Malala Yousafzai, a woman who, from an extremely young age, fought against the Taliban to promote girls' rights to education. She was fearless in the face of harassment and even death threats, anchored by surety in her cause. In 2012, at the tender age of fifteen, she wrote:

> "We human beings don't realize how great God is. He has given us an extraordinary brain and a sensitive loving heart. He has blessed us with two lips to talk and express our feelings, two eyes which see a world of colors and beauty, two feet which walk on the road of life, two hands to work for us, and two ears to hear the words of love" (Lamb 2013, 421).

She has been successful not only because of her gift with words but because she so clearly shows a love for all of humanity. Her courage is bolstered by a bone-deep belief in people's capacity for goodness to overcome the demons of our lesser nature. In other words, Malala demonstrates agape, and that has made her strong.

These people show us love is simply an inner virtue directed outward. They are great figures who will echo through history because their agape—their love for all people regardless of personal differences or former actions—effected positive change in the world.

Showing love for people you don't know is the ultimate expression of inner virtue. Acts of charity, helping people before they ask, and building bridges between groups who are at odds with one another are signs of true strength of character. When sharing your agape with the world, you reveal the best of yourself, the kernel of goodness at your center. You LOVE. *You let your virtue emerge.*

CHAPTER 2

The Ethics of Agape

Picking apart the implications of an outlook such as agape requires questioning certain extreme moral possibilities. Does any situation or circumstance exist in which we should not show unconditional love toward our fellow human beings? Love is probably the most potent and polarizing emotion people feel and can be a motivator for actions both supremely virtuous and totally flawed. Questions naturally arise. Can a person ever do something to make them no longer deserving of love? When does love lead to weakness in the face of danger? Ethics enters in when considering these obstacles. History, logic, or even common sense relays that, virtuous intentions aside, sometimes strength needs to be met with strength.

One of the central tenets of agape is a focus on charity, self-sacrifice, and generally prioritizing the well-being of others over your own self. It involves doing good without expecting anything in return. But what is the limit? Asking anyone to unconditionally commit every aspect of their life to the property of others seems like a tall order and is an unnuanced and wholly incorrect interpretation of agape. The vital question then becomes, at what degree does agape become unacceptable? When showing love for others results in harm to yourself, where should you draw the line?

The Bible seems to indicate agape is a virtue to be prized above all others and does not often qualify it. It exists in numerous places within the holy book, but scholars typically agree that the spirit of agape lives most clearly in the well-known biblical passage:

> "Thou shalt love the Lord thy God with all thy heart, and with all thy soul, and with all thy mind. This is the first and great commandment. And second is like unto it, thou shalt love thy neighbor as thyself. On these two commandments hang all the law and the prophets." (Matt. 22:37-40 KJV).

However, while the Bible promotes the value of love countless times, it still leaves us with a question of degree. Matters of principle are straightforward to advocate for in general, but specific determinations can get trickier. This idea is demonstrated in the common philosophical premise of stealing is morally wrong but feeding your family is morally right. So, is stealing a loaf of bread to feed your family morally right? Great thinkers across time have gone back and forth on questions like this and have so far only proven the questions are difficult to answer.

In *Agape: An Ethical Analysis*, Gene Outka writes, "These are well-worn but notoriously difficult questions whose almost obstinate longevity among sophisticated and unsophisticated alike suggests how deeply they are felt and how inescapable they are in ethical reflection" (Outka 1977, 9). Questions on the ethical bounds of service to others— "How much do I owe other people?"—have stumped human beings for centuries.

Before we as individuals can even attempt to answer those questions, we must develop our own views on the ethics of agape. When should we show agape, and when should we not? Whatever our definition of morality, we all have our own baseline for what's acceptable, both in our behavior toward others and in their behavior toward us.

To help us hone in on that baseline, the simplest and most important thing to remember is we are all human. We all make mistakes. This applies not only to us but to everyone around us. Even when we do not approach others from a place of forgiveness and grace, we are often surprised, enraged, or offended when someone does the same to us. When we react negatively to every little slight, we can end up with the mindset that we can do no wrong, which is a dangerous belief because it further limits our ability to love others when we experience conflict. We may not have the opportunity to listen to everyone, to learn their story and the motivations behind their actions, but we can remind ourselves to respect them the way we hope they will respect us. This means controlling our negative thoughts and letting go of our judgment. Not every slight is intentional, and even if it is, in many situations, it's not important. If we can change our thoughts about the situation and resist approaching people from a place of judgment, we will find it easier to remain calm and avoid making their problems our own.

Some people are able to reach a place where they can practice agape in all situations. They are able to accept that not everyone will respond positively to their kindness—that some people will still approach them with hate. In many of those cases, the person showing agape is still stronger for it. They've developed their own sense of morality that benefits them and their lives, and they are able to accept that the love they show will sometimes not be returned or even acknowledged.

For others, however, acceptance of another person's hate is more difficult. It is excessively simplistic to encourage a person to turn over their life to the service of others without any regard for what that would do to them personally. There are times when it is difficult or potentially dangerous to continue showing love to someone. An example is in cases of abuse. How do we reconcile loving someone in such a situation? Sometimes, sacrificing our own needs, happiness, and feelings of self-worth becomes impossible. Everyone has limits, and when you reach those limits, the idea of agape must shift from showing love to people who hurt you to showing love to yourself.

I always had a difficult relationship with my mother. When I was a child, she became angry over small inconveniences, which led to her being verbally abusive. When I was five and learning to write, I asked my mother for help with the letter z, but she was cooking dinner and didn't want to be bothered. She lost her temper and cussed at me, telling me to do it myself. This behavior continued throughout my life into adulthood. Is my mother all bad, no this I know for sure. She has helped me greatly in my life. Over time, I decided that treatment was unacceptable, and I walked away, choosing to love myself first. When loving another comes at the cost of your safety, well-being, and self-esteem, walking away may be the only option.

Whether or not abuse or other trauma is involved, there is no one definitive response to the question of how far to take agape in all its varied forms. Everyone is in a different position to commit themselves to charity, forgiveness, friendship, and all the other nuances of agape. Simply, agape begins and ends at different places for different people. This is far too complex a question for an objective, across-the-board solution.

CHAPTER 3

American Life

American life is plagued by a lack of love, and that problem has manifested in many forms. Politically, the country is more divided now than during any period of time since the Civil War, and it's not hard to see why. The war on drugs has mutated into a targeted takedown of race and class, and the war on terror has taken freedom and privacy from many Americans. The uptick in fatal shootings is possibly the most alarming of all, resulting in forty-nine thousand deaths in the United States in 2021 alone (Giffords 2022). People everywhere, most of whom are doing their best to help, can't agree on basic choices in government and politics. This has resulted in congressional gridlock and inaction or overreaction in situations in which a timely but well-considered response is crucial.

Shootings in schools, churches, movie theaters, and more continue to manifest every week, always accompanied by the all-too-familiar refrain of "thoughts and prayers" from political figures expressing concern they don't seem to feel. While politicians and think tanks waffle about possible fixes and the nature of the problem, solutions are never enacted. Meanwhile, cemeteries nationwide are peppered with the graves of targets, and far too many families are left diminished.

Whatever a person's political persuasion, nobody denies these events are tragedies. However, one thing people have failed to consider about the mass shootings problem—along with most of the issues society faces today—is that in order to solve a problem, we must find the root of it first. Could it be that the debate on gun control is centered around the wrong question? Maybe we are asking, "How can this be stopped?" too much, instead of, "Why is this happening at all?"

What drives mass shooters to do what they do? Why would someone ever be motivated to commit such a blatant act of destruction? Sometimes the perpetrator suggests a reason for their behavior. It might be bigotry, an act of terror, mental illness, or simply a deeply misguided desire to stand out. We should never fall victim to the resigned assumptions that "they were just made that way," "it was inevitable—that person was never going to be normal," and the like. Such things are never true, not of anyone. We all come into this world ready to love, but those who are unloved, manipulated, or grow up in an environment of hate have that feeling muted and even disconnected. People who are corrupted by cruelty, through no fault of their own, lack the sense of love, allowing them to commit terrible crimes—often without remorse. It's a tragedy many of those people are never able to be rehabilitated, but there are those who find their way out of that darkness and commit to changing themselves for the better.

Life After Hate, an organization dedicated to helping neo-Nazis and white nationalists find love and understanding for all people, is one of the great modern American examples of this attitude. Former far-right extremists founded the movement in 2011, with a mission to "[inspire] individuals to a place of compassion and forgiveness for everyone, including themselves" (The Good Times 2017). Life After Hate is fighting an uphill battle, but the organization's successes are heartening. They have changed the minds of felons convicted of hate crimes—extremist organizers and lifelong white supremacists, all people who almost certainly would have continued to spread hate for the rest of their lives—and, maybe more importantly, have done their best to convince a new generation of Americans to think in a similar way. This organization shows anyone is capable of choosing agape.

It's naïve to think we can prevent all tragedies. Although many people can learn to love through agape, some will choose not to. It's hard to change your approach toward other people, especially when hatred for those who are different from you has been normalized. However, love is contagious, and agape can help us recover from the tragedies that do occur and find a better way forward. An important question to ask is, "How can we avoid creating more people who have no connection to love?" Finding the answer will take a lot of time and work, not only because it is difficult to create that kind of change on a large scale, but because it needs to start on an individual level. Agape is all-powerful in the hands of people united in working to create a better world.

Agape should extend to everyone, including those who wrong others, but that will be a difficult hurdle for many to overcome. Loving people who commit violent and hateful acts is difficult. Violence and prejudice are powerful tools, and they expertly weave a web of lies, convincing us those people are incapable of reshaping their ways. These terrible forces drive us apart, polarize us, frighten us, and radicalize us at great cost to the world.

America's response to the September 11 terrorist attacks is indicative of the harm that can come when you meet a vicious attack with equal malice, but it also shows the power of love to help us recover in a time of such pain and loss. Many people found comfort in prayer, community, and family, and they made it through the terror stronger because they relied on love to counter reckless hate. They grieved the fallen and continued with their lives. They did not forget what transpired on 9/11, but they endured. When it would have been easy to collapse and despair that anyone would do something so despicable, people soldiered on. They did not fall to wondering why some people are so hardened against love, nor how someone could commit such a terrible crime. They showed the best of America in those dark days.

However, some people used these attacks as a reason to hate. They didn't find a foundation for greater strength through love and unity, just flimsy excuses to raise the specter of Islamophobia that remains today. Bias is the surest way to splinter the unity of people opposing the madness of terrorism, and many people fell prey to that instinct. But agape is love for everyone. Damning an entire religion, nearly two billion people, for the actions of a few radicals is a failure of great significance.

Though some people stood up for those being targeted because of this bias, an unfortunate segment of Americans reacted to 9/11 with mistrust and prejudice toward Muslims and people from the Middle East. It is understandable some people would turn in this direction. Blaming someone is an easy way to divert pain and fear onto a tangible source. Casting people who are different from you as villains doesn't require strenuous thought, forgiveness, or understanding. Hate is insidious like that. It is the siren song following a tragedy. Hate pretends to offer a simple solution to inevitable confusion following great strife, a clear-cut worldview that ostensibly will make it easier to deal with heartbreak. But the peace hate promises is a lie. The satisfaction that soothes you in the short term is merely an illusion. Hate tears you up inside and causes you to lash out, spreading pain and hate to others. It spreads like a virus.

Though it is difficult, don't turn to hate after a fresh wound. Hatred will force your pain deeper and can only be stopped by love and understanding. We must use agape to reprogram the way we look at tragedy and misfortune. But how can we do that when judgment and hate are so ingrained in society? It's not as easy as just choosing to love others. We have to figure out the root of the issue, the cause of such hate, and learn what we personally can do to take action against it.

CHAPTER 4

Practicing Love in Everyday Life

Learning to love those who are different from us begins with understanding why it's so easy to hate. Humans have an innate need to categorize things to make sense of the world. During our evolution, that categorization was necessary for survival. Now, however, it manifests as categorizing other people—separating them into "like us" or "not like us." This can easily lead to stereotyping, which can cause generalizations and misunderstanding. If we perceive a person as belonging to a group we can't identify with, we may fail to see them as an individual, and when we assign those group characteristics to a specific person, we can end up making assumptions about them that are often unfair and untrue.

Because we have a tendency to fear what is different, if we believe those differences pose a threat to us, we will react with anger. In many cases, that reaction can keep us safe. However, if we know we are not actually in danger, allowing our anger to get the best of us is harmful, not only to others but to ourselves. In everyday situations—if we're cut off in traffic or have a disagreement with someone—there are strategies we can employ to help us act from a place of love, which will naturally allow us to overcome our anger.

In the New International Bible, 1 Peter 4:8 reads, "Above all, love each other deeply, because love covers a multitude of sins." This is a major theme throughout the Bible. Love and charity should be the driving forces behind your thoughts and actions. Going beyond loving our family and friends, we should endeavor to love each person we meet. Think of a time when the random kindness of a stranger made your day better. Try to remember your reaction—not only how you felt but how you acted toward others following the initial interaction. This is a point on which psychologists, sociologists, the Quran, and the Bible all concur: people are more positive toward others after receiving positivity themselves. Each act builds to another, and another, and another.

Loving everyone can clearly benefit your life and the lives of those you care for—but that message often loses steam when translated from lofty fantasy to real-life effort. Progressing from thoughts of love to carrying out positive deeds and holding an open, welcoming disposition toward everyone—including your biggest enemies—can be a difficult transition for many people. It begins with small changes, things we can enact in our everyday lives.

Let's say, after putting this book down, you realize the fridge is getting empty and decide to go grocery shopping. While en route to the store, another driver swerves in front of you while talking on their phone, clearly not looking out for anyone else on the road. This is probably someone you have never met, a person who holds no ill will toward you personally but who was just not considering their actions. This driver cutting you off in traffic doesn't even inconvenience you that much, but you overreact and judge the person based on one incident.

It's a natural human reaction and nothing to be ashamed of; most people have strong impulse responses to everyday nuisances.

Behavioral psychologists have studied similar patterns of interactions and found the average person responds to certain nuisances—of which stubbing your toe is another common example—with a disproportionate level of impulse for a specific reason. When something entirely out of your control impacts you negatively, your brain doesn't have enough time to process the event itself. Thus, it bypasses normal emotional checks and moves straight to an anger response. Many people can control those feelings, but for those with anger problems, the struggle to calm down after the inciting event is more difficult. Intense negative emotions cloud your judgment, making it harder to find a solution. Have you ever been late, trying to find a set of keys in a cluttered house? Finding those keys will be easier every time if you stop, calm down, and try to think clearly. Clear thinking is impossible if you are angry or contemptuous.

Something that may help us react differently in negative situations involving other people is remembering these people, like us, are focused on their own needs. This is sonder, the realization every person we encounter is living their own full and complex life, just like we are. While our primary focus is what's going on in our own lives and hearts, the same is true of every other person we see. Knowing this can make it easier to understand that person's perspective, and it may remind us to think before we react negatively, giving ourselves the few seconds needed to regain control. It can allow us to realize that, while the person's needs may conflict with our own, we are not necessarily right, nor them wrong. It's easy to make snap judgments, but part of agape is learning how to look past those judgments so it becomes easier to control our reactions to and thoughts about others.

Another strategy to help curb negative emotions and the instinct to respond to unpleasant behavior in kind is to remember, in most cases, people's actions toward you—the things they do and say about you—are more about their relationship with themselves than their relationship with you. People deflect personal confrontation onto interactions with others all the time. The stress from unpaid bills is easy to redirect toward a stranger. So, when others treat you poorly, remind yourself their actions are likely a result of other stressors in their life and their poor ability to cope with those stressors. When you understand other people are dealing with issues unknown to you, being altruistic in every aspect of your behavior, even toward people who seem to want to hurt you and bring you down, will become a much simpler task.

Like everyone else, I have encountered this in my own life. I remember a time years ago, before I came up with LOVE, when I was at the grocery store. An older woman in front of me buying collard greens argued with the cashier about the price. Her concern seemed so small and petty to me, and I grew impatient and made judgments about her based on this one incident, simply because I didn't want to wait. Later, I lost my job and was on food stamps. When I went to the store and tried to buy a rotisserie chicken, I found out they weren't covered. I was going to put it back, but the cashier bought it for me. That act of kindness, while it may seem small to many people, had a huge impact on me. It helped me realize the power of being understanding and forgiving and that the kindness the cashier extended to me was something I should have extended to the lady who'd been in front of me and other people around me.

Later on in my life, one of my friends was struggling and asked to borrow money. I didn't have any to give, but when I learned she needed it for groceries and gas, I took the opportunity to show agape, to extend that goodness to her. I explained to her I did not have cash but I did have a credit card, and I told her to meet me at the gas station and grocery store. Then I used my credit card to help her get what she needed. I approached her situation from a place of agape. These experiences show that embracing an attitude of agape can keep us from spiraling out of control when facing challenges in life or offenses by other people—big or small.

The presence of love has the ability to drive out petty differences and make any slight negligible. Living a life filled with love means making compassion, charity, trust, and altruism part of your daily behavior. Forgiveness should not be a rare instance for you. When you walk down the street, seek out what you have in common with people, not the things that are different. If you practice the ideal of goodwill toward all people, if you take that notion to heart and internalize it, if you truly feel the primal connection we all have with one another, you will find petty judgments and useless negative emotions have less impact on you. The man who cuts you off in traffic while talking on his phone, the woman who bumps into you on the street because she is texting and who doesn't apologize, the person in the laundromat who tosses your wet clothes on the floor to use the washing machine for themselves, the person who doesn't hold the door for you—rather than thinking these people are in some way out to get you, you'll realize they are simply loved ones you haven't met and they deserve to be treated with compassion.

The world is filled with cynics. Many people are entrenched in the notion that their fellow humans are unintelligent, uncaring, or cannot be relied upon to do the right thing. However, when you take the time to understand people, why they do what they do, their pasts and their futures, it becomes impossible not to feel a sense of kinship and even love. That is agape, and you must care for it and nourish it within everything you do. When you are full of love, you will cherish each person for their humanity and their virtues, seen and unseen. As more people adopt this outlook, a new world of peace and happiness will bloom.

PART 2

What Happens to People When They Are Deprived of Love

CHAPTER 5

The Profound Impacts of Lacking Love

While the benefits, great and small, of practicing a lifestyle centered around love for others are clear, the costs of a total lack of love are equally apparent. Just as helping others and working to make a better world can improve your life, working to worsen someone's life—even someone who has done wrong and arguably deserves it—will bring suffering into your life. What motivates you becomes your center, your focal point around which all emotions and behaviors develop, so internalizing malice will only lead to more bad feelings. Hate, like love, grows the more it's practiced.

An idiom that encapsulates this thought pattern is: "Holding on to anger is like drinking poison and expecting another person to die." When hate lives inside your heart, it does nothing but perpetuate hate. It infects the person holding on to the malicious feelings and influences that person's actions. That, in turn, affects how others act, and not in a positive way. When you show hatred toward someone, they may be more likely to respond in the same manner. To combat this issue, people must be able to move their anger from inside and quell the impulse to find someone to blame.

Though altruism opens your mind to new possibilities and helps you see the world from different points of view, finding empathy for anyone remotely different from you is a monumental task. Life is not so cut-and-dried. Most people live in shades of gray, doing some good and some bad. In order to improve ourselves in that respect, we must remember dehumanizing other people, whether it's because they've wronged us or simply because they have different beliefs, does not make anything better, no matter the intention. Dislike and lack of compassion for the world only serve to diminish a person's worldview and narrow the spectrum of their judgment. Entrenched beliefs lead to a halt in social progress at best and extremism at worst.

This is the case all over the world and throughout history. Every never-ending religious clash, protracted political conflict, and racial or ethnic struggle is founded in hatred and an unwillingness or inability to see things from another person's point of view. An example is from the Middle Ages, when millions of Christians and Muslims died during the Crusades—a series of wars for control of the Holy Land, what is now Israel, Jordan, and sections of Lebanon and Syria. For hundreds of years, the sacred area was polluted by conflict, and the engagements ultimately had little effect on control of the region. Two faiths, both based on ideals of peace and brotherhood, found hatred in their differences, and death quickly followed. Blindness brought on by ignorance and intolerance is a scourge on humanity, and it has already claimed the hearts and lives of too many innocent people.

Unfortunately, there seems to be an increasing distance between people in everyday life. The term "stranger" is growing more literal as time goes on. The differences that make each individual unique become excuses to forget about those who are not part of our little bubble of existence. Algorithms on social media create echo chambers online. Instead of bringing us closer together, they segment and categorize, weeding out the voices we don't want to hear. In these situations, someone may feel comfortable in the belief that they are a good, accepting, and tolerant person. Love may seem to come naturally. However, it is easy to love everyone you see when you limit your field of vision to people who are similar. While bonding through shared experiences and values is positive, it can sometimes lead to the belief that a person unlike us is not worth our time or consideration. Instead of being open to the beauty and enormity of life's potential, we seal ourselves off and create a limited worldview that makes ignorant, selfish choices feel natural and justifiable.

Even when we do have the opportunity to engage in discourse with those who are different from us, too many people use that as an excuse to pile hate and judgment on to others. That has been made easier than ever before through the emergence and popularity of social media. People who would never share certain thoughts in real life, perhaps out of a fear of judgment or confrontation, are free to say whatever they think without the risk of any real consequences. The security created online by anonymity and the feeling of being safe behind their keyboard emboldens people to proclaim opinions they would otherwise have no opportunity to share with anyone outside their own circle. They have a larger platform, more people to speak to, without even having to leave their computer. While social media could be used to bring us together, it often leads to more and more people showing the darker parts of themselves—the hatred they may hide in their everyday lives.

Seeing so many instances of anger and hatred can be discouraging, and it's easy to respond in kind rather than take the opportunity to be understanding and approach people from a place of love. A lot of our ideas of right and wrong are ingrained in us from childhood, and unfortunately, many people are raised in environments that encourage judgment and hatred. Rather than continuing this cycle, each person needs to make the choice to break it. Enough problems arise naturally without us creating more. We must learn to treat each other as brothers and sisters, put aside grievances and the weight of history, and overcome biases too long nurtured by laziness and convenience to face the multitude of challenges life provides.

It's difficult to know where to start when trying to lead a life more full of love. A good practice is to notice what instances in our lives bring out our tendency toward judgment and anger and find new ways to approach them. In some cases, that approach may be to simply walk away. If we are inclined to join arguments online, we could choose not to engage in them, not to share our opinions, no matter how much we may disagree with someone and want to make them see from our perspective. While this may not feel like agape, it is actually showing love to ourselves by protecting ourselves from our own tendency to react unkindly. It gives us the opportunity to step away from an unpleasant situation before we lash out. It also shows love to those our words could potentially hurt. Sometimes, when we're focused on trying to change someone else's mind, we forget their thoughts and experiences are valid, too. We forget that how we feel when someone is cruel to us is likely how they feel when we do the same. Stopping that behavior before it begins can help us learn the self-control needed to practice agape in instances where conflict is unavoidable.

While each individual working to understand others may not be able to solve the world's problems, it is a great place to start. A core of goodwill is what effectively changes the world. That positive energy, directed toward evil in the world, is how we win with love.

PART 3

How We Can Improve Our Lives and the Lives of Others by Being More Loving

CHAPTER 6

Love as a Teacher

Love can build a better world in numerous ways, and one of the most important steps in the process is teaching and bettering children. People, none more so than kids, learn by example. If we want to get rid of hate, violence, and destruction, educating the next generation is the key. Showing people how to live without hate can temper crimes before they happen and discourage threats from being carried out. It can reduce that flash of anger and lessen petty bickering. When kids grow up learning that anger and dislike are completely dysfunctional outlets for confusion and frustration, the world will have a shot at peace.

But before we can teach others, we must learn ourselves. Internal reflection—examining our own biases and reactions and where they come from—is necessary to get us to a place where our experience can be beneficial to others. If we preach agape but do not show it in our everyday lives, the concept may feel like empty words. Showing others kindness, love, and forgiveness is the only way to get them to truly understand. The course forward is simple. Mother Teresa, a missionary sainted by the Catholic Church, said it well: "Spread love wherever you go. Let no one come to you without leaving happier" (Costello 2009, 21). Do your best, every day, to react to each of life's surprises, both pleasant and unpleasant, with those words in mind, and everyone around you will benefit by example.

Life will always provide opportunities to impart this lesson. Remember the strategies you learned earlier in the book and use those when you find yourself getting angry or impatient. Whenever you are presented with someone who says or does something that comes across as unfeeling or makes your life harder, stop and imagine the situation from their position. How might your actions look to another person? If you're chastised at work, maybe the other person can't see the full scope of your situation, through no fault of their own. More importantly, maybe they are projecting their problems or insecurities on to your life. Or maybe they don't have control over the situation and you are unfairly blaming them.

People routinely apply these patterns of behavior to one another. We have all made the same mistakes as everyone around us and will undoubtedly make them again. Knowing that, try to react to other people with agape in your heart. Continue to hold a forgiving attitude, and soon, people will respond to you with kindness. If this happens enough, a societal shift won't be far away.

An act of agape that led to one of these shifts was when Dr. Martin Luther King Jr. effectively forged the American Civil Rights Movement on notions of nonviolence and peaceful protesting. There was great anger on both sides, but his approach was founded on agape. Whereas some saw racists and bigots—people who were irredeemable and broken, inextricably tied to an unfair system that raised them up—Dr. King saw people who were misguided. He saw people who had been fed poison for generations; and when people are raised on poison, they inevitably seek more. He even saw, to some degree, victims—people who had inherited a disease from their fathers and their fathers' fathers. With that outlook, love is far easier, and nonviolent resistance is the obvious choice. He famously said, "Darkness cannot drive out darkness; only light can do that. Hate cannot drive out hate; only love can do that" (King 1964, 45). Every generation should carry that approach with them when dealing with strong opposition and even evil. Whether a simple political disagreement, a blatant and selfish lie, or even a terrible crime, hate cannot be our response. Hate will only perpetuate a cycle of hate. It will only feed opponents the poison on which they have been raised. Nobody is born racist. Nobody is born a murderer or a despot. They are our brothers and sisters, despite any infractions. And, through persistence, agape will see we are united.

However, we must remember that even when we understand the concept of showing agape—where it comes from, why it's important, and how to do it—actually putting it into practice is difficult, especially in an environment that doesn't seem to care about being loving or empathetic. American society encourages being reactionary. While that makes for effective entertainment sometimes, whether on TV or in real life, it often leads to unhappiness for the people involved. Not tempering basic impulses can be satisfying. It can be comforting to believe you are absolutely right and "the other side" is entirely wrong, casting your opponents as one-sided villains with no point or purpose other than to serve as objects of your displeasure. In simplifying the world to such a degree, you can avoid tricky concepts such as self-doubt and inward scrutiny. Life is easier with a viewpoint like that.

However, understanding your views on the world shouldn't be easy. Considering opposing viewpoints shouldn't be simple. Maintaining an honest view of other people and issues should be a complex process with no fortune-cookie wisdom to easily summarize what you believe about nuanced issues of today's import and why you believe what you do. In order to do that, it's important to avoid making generalizations and judgments about groups of people unlike us. We package people's political affiliations with preassembled notions about their character, morality, and even sanity. As discussed in chapter 5, children are growing up in an online-dominated world, leading to a lack of love in real life. And while the reality of this is tragic, it's also a chance to encourage tremendous improvement. Every day, they encounter scenarios they can resolve in either an approachable, healthy manner devoid of malice and senseless judgement or from an unquestioning point of view that dulls critical thinking and empathy. How they approach these situations will depend on how they're taught and the examples of behavior they have around them.

If a child is at school and another kid makes fun of them for getting an answer wrong in front of the class, this is an opportunity for growth, not only for the child but for our entire culture. Unfortunately, too many people don't see it that way. They either don't want to work to change their behavior or, especially in the case of children, don't realize the behavior needs to be changed because it's been normalized by those around them. But while children learn much of their beliefs from their parents and guardians, they also see what other people do. Modeling good behavior can show them that coming from a place of love and forgiveness can reduce conflicts and negative feelings.

Some children do have the opportunity to grow up in that kind of caring environment. A kid with a good upbringing, not only from their parents and family but from everyone around them, may be less likely to respond to aggression from their peers because they've developed the strength to not take it personally. Nurturing, agape-centered childhoods foster people who are not only sympathetic but confident enough not to succumb to pettiness and personal assaults. They can be brave and aware to the degree that unfriendly words won't matter. In turn, they can model this behavior for other children, who may not have encountered it anywhere else. If enough kids begin learning from that example, it will spread and perhaps help some of them temper their negative impulses before they move into adulthood, when it is arguably more difficult to change our thought processes. If children bear in mind that aggression says far more about the aggressor than it does about them, hostility won't beget hostility. Keep in mind, however, that it is as important for children to understand the limits of agape as it is for adults. They should never be taught they must put up with abuse to make someone else happy. We need to teach them when it is okay to turn that love toward themselves instead of others.

When you learn to see through a person's chance infractions to the individual underneath, you won't react harshly. In this way, the cycle of trivial bickering will break, and that is a huge step forward. When people grow up learning to not respond to negativity with more negativity, they will also cease to start similar actions themselves. Casual negativity won't consume our reality. Resentment will recede. People will have healthier relationships and more productive lives. In short, the world will improve, all through the power of empathy and agape.

If eliminating small responses to small insults does not seem important, try to see the whole picture. Politeness to one another is often an undervalued practice, one that should be emphasized to a much greater degree. As is true in every endeavor, the little things are the foundations to greater change. Graciousness and civility—such as holding the door for someone or consistently saying thank you—are reminders that the people surrounding us, especially strangers, are human as well. They aren't background characters simply there to populate our world; they are individuals with personalities, ambitions, problems, situations, and circumstances. Treating them as nonentities is dehumanizing and can lead to much greater acts of negativity.

Once you stop yielding to pedestrians or being understanding of a cashier who says your coupon has expired, you start to desensitize yourself to their humanity. This numbing clears a path for worse actions than small arguments or a bad day at work. It leads to fights, biases, and pain. Disregarding the experiences and feelings of the individuals around you is the first step toward doing the same to whole groups of people, most of whom you've never met. Suddenly, you're wrongly blaming them for bigger problems. Then politics gets involved, and unfair policies are enacted. Brick by brick, the issue builds until innocent people are hurting. Countries go to war. All this springs from simple acts of dehumanization on a small, personal scale.

Once you open your eyes to the power of living a life centered around agape, people who are dissimilar to you can enrich your experiences and even give you a clearer picture of yourself. It will become easier to accept that other people are much more than facets of your life, playing a role in your existence. They have stories of their own. They are flesh-and-blood individuals going through life as you are. Treat them as such and teach children to treat them as such. Allow the next generation to grow up in a world in which no one is faceless and no group is uniform. Teach them everyone is unique and deserving of love and agape.

Love for others can be the difference between a good life and a great life. Knowing and accepting other people and acknowledging the extensive gamut of human experiences will help you be a more thoughtful and understanding person. When you feel a connection with every person around you, you open yourself to the limitless possibilities and depth life can provide, both good and bad.

Conclusion

How do we make an ideal world full of agape love a reality? There isn't a concrete step to bring everything together in one fell swoop. Our world doesn't convert to anything en masse. Major change takes time and sustained effort, so we must be clear and united in how we direct our energy; it begins with everyone doing their part.

If history shows us anything, it's that the only plausible way to act out of love, compassion, and a sense of agape for someone else is to hold it in ourselves and express it in our actions. Seeing another person act with kindness and forgiveness, especially in situations in which they are often difficult to find, demonstrates to the world that kindness and forgiveness are possible.

The good part about this verdict is that everybody is personally in control of their part. Your contribution—the expression of compassion and even love for strangers who have wronged you—to a more agape-filled world is entirely in your power. The hard part is that although this concept is simple enough, it is not easy to practice. Compassion is often extremely difficult. It often feels like the wrong response. Anger toward and reprisals against someone who has wronged you might be the easiest path, while compassion is often treated like weakness. If someone insults you, the easiest and perhaps most natural response is to respond in the same manner. Only people committed to building a more peaceful and compassionate life will realize such a response only encourages further conflict. "An eye for an eye makes the whole world blind" is a well-known but little-observed truism, and while those stakes are considerably higher than the small problems and fights most people end up in, the proverb is no less correct.

Only through combined will and unity of purpose can lasting, positive shifts be made. Through extensive focus on self-control, people can make a difference, not only in their own lives but in the lives of people around them. It can and does happen all the time, but each of us needs to be willing to put in the work to get there.

This book has a fair share of doom and gloom in it, so let's shift gears. While most of us drift somewhere in the nebulous landscape of positivity, mostly good but sometimes straying into the bounds of cynicism, distrust, and even degradation, there are people—everyone knows at least a few—who consistently, and almost relentlessly, remain positive. These are people who never have something bad to say about someone else, who brush off all the vain insults and petty comments they're confronted with—in short, people who display all the qualities and temperament of those who believe in the philosophy of agape. These are people who truly let their virtue emerge, or LOVE.

These people often stand out because there aren't many like them. They have learned to LOVE in a way many haven't. We admire them for their kindness and compassion, but often that's as far as it goes. We don't try to follow their lead too hard or for too long. Maybe it's because we don't think we can, or we worry it will turn us into doormats and welcome abuse. Maybe we don't think a lifestyle so full of empathy and consideration would be interesting. After all, how many reality TV shows, video games, or even gossip sessions with our friends stand in opposition to empathy and consideration?

Those are understandable reasons for not always being the best we could be. But what if, instead of offering a few easy compliments to these people who are always positive and kind, we tried to emulate them? What if we tried to be like that woman from work who never dishes out gossip or that guy we went to school with who would always step up for someone who was getting made fun of? What if we didn't indulge in the minor nastiness that seems to be growing in everyday life? What if we let our virtue emerge?

That virtue exists in everyone. Though there's no definitive answer to the question of whether we're born with empathy or learn it throughout our lives, many human beings, despite erring often, want to help and love one another. We don't go through life wanting to hurt, but for many people, it is easier to hurt unintentionally because they are hurt themselves. It takes work, but we are capable of changing that tendency, of coming from the place of compassion we wish others would approach us from.

This type of change is undoubtedly hard, and bigger, more substantive forgiveness for greater slights is even more difficult. However, the results would be impressive. Combating jealousy, dislike, and uncaringness can make a world of difference. Bringing agape to the forefront of our guiding moral compass and exhibiting love for our fellow human beings as our lodestar—these actions can change the world.

It's not always easy to practice agape, but when you make yourself an example of this behavior, you'll see people all around you respond. The more people respond, the more an atmosphere of kindness and patience will grow, and that, in turn, will engender more people to adapt their behavior around agape. In words that have echoed across generations, Gandhi is often quoted as saying, "Be the change you wish to see in the world." If our goal is to create a more universal, loving world, we have to begin by embracing and embodying those values ourselves. We begin with LOVE. *Let our virtue emerge.*

BONUS CHAPTER

Early Scholarship on Love

For millennia, great thinkers, philosophers, psychologists, and neurologists have attempted to uncover the true nature of love in all its forms, love's place in our lives, and how people interact with it. We—mostly nonexperts living in the modern world—create our conception of love from a combination of interpretations from these sources and how they have seeped into our lives through familial teaching and interpersonal experience. While these individualistic notions are perfectly valid, it is worth examining the more focused, academic, conceptions.

One pillar of our cultural conception of love is philosophy, not because we all spend time reading historical texts or listening to theoretical discussions about love but because we are shaped by the countless generations before us, and at some point, the people of those generations were directly shaped by grand philosophical debates.

Philosophers approach the topic through principles of pure reason—that is, they pursue the question, "How does love logically fit in with the rest of the world?" To go all the way back to the roots of Western philosophy, we need to discuss the Greek philosophers. The Greeks grouped all types of love together under the umbrella of eros. That idea includes not only the focus of this book, agape, but also other types, such as erotic love and romantic love. Counter to some widespread misconceptions, many Greek philosophers understood love as a concept that could be discretely divided, not as a uniform and mostly selfish emotion.

Early Greeks did often view love as inherently inward facing. For them, love for someone else was actually love for what that person could bring to them and not something unselfish or incurious. Similarly, love and devotion to their gods was love and devotion to spiritual satisfaction, as opposed to true religious fervor for a higher power. Finally, of course, while they believed in the power of kindred spirits and brotherhood, they would not have called it love but an attachment to something similar to them and the protection it could bring.

However, later Greek thinkers were not as single-minded. In Platonic Eros and Christian Agape, well-known English scholar and professor of Greek studies A. H. Armstrong wrote, "An increasing number of people who have seriously studied Plato . . . are increasingly dissatisfied with the sharp antithesis between Greek philosophical eros and Christian *agape* which was given currency (previously) . . . They maintain that [scholars] have failed to grasp the depth, range and value of the conception of eros in Plato and later Platonists" (Armstrong 1961, 105). He goes on to cover how Plato and later thinkers massively expanded beyond early Greek scholars and their views on the single-minded nature of love.

Of course, numerous later thinkers, notably Roman philosophers Plutarch and Cicero, worked to discourage Platonic ideas of love as the fanciful concepts common in Greek culture. Roman notions of love centered squarely on marriage in general. However, as years passed, Christian philosophers started to gain traction, not only in Rome but around the Western world.

One major figure in the birth of this new school of thought was Saint Augustine of Hippo, a Numidian citizen of Rome who drew on early Biblical study, Judaean teachings, and even Greek scholarship to form his body of work. Augustine famously wrote "there is no entrance into truth except through love" and "to fall in love with God is the greatest romance." He indicated that devotion and love for God would connect you to "all of his children." This early conception of agape set many other Christian philosophers down similar paths.

The most notable beneficiary of Saint Augustine was perhaps Saint Thomas Aquinas, who, although born many centuries later, based much of his work on Augustinian teachings. Aquinas believed love was the only rational center of a system of ethics because it was the only way to truly praise God. He did not separate his moral life from his spiritual life. He believed the former to be based completely on the latter.

In *The Primacy of Love: An Introduction to the Ethics of Thomas Aquinas*, Paul Wadell writes, "The overall purpose of the moral life was to make us the kind of people whose lives are a song of praise to a God whose love is unending. [Aquinas] knew the moral life is the Christian life, that to grow in goodness is to be transfigured in holiness, and that charity is no idle love, but is the virtue that makes life an offering to God" (Wadell 2009). Thomas Aquinas was an ardent believer in love as the foundation of his faith, and his faith as the foundation of all charity and other good works.

Other philosophers' notions of love followed the same paths as Aquinas's and Augustine's, although their religion was less a part of their conclusions. One such scholar was the French philosopher Emmanuel Levinas, who fervently believed in the social ethics of love. Simply put, Levinas saw love for one another as the force that held a functioning society together. This was not just love for family members or even close friends but a broader and more abstract love for fellow citizens, not in a self-involved way but rather for the specific differences that branched off of what made people similar.

In *Philosophy and Love: From Plato to Popular Culture*, Linnell Secomb writes:

> The relation of love emerges as a crucial element in the ethical reflection of the French philosopher, Emmanuel Levinas. For Levinas, the personal, ethical, and political relation between the self and the other is central: those relations are found on or conditioned by love. For Levinas the inter-human relation . . . is the most important philosophical issue . . . this formulation of our ethical responsibility is intertwined in various crucial ways, in Levinas's work . . . for Levinas, all ethical social relations are an expression of love" (Secomb 2007, 59).

Of course, most of our interhuman relations are with people we do not know well at all, and Levinas would say ethical behavior in those relations is an expression of love. His work therefore supports agape, even though notions of spirituality or a higher power do not enter into it.

Following Levinas, scholarship on love continued to branch off in countless directions. More modern scholarship about love has been increasingly independent of religion than in years past. Some scholars have even fused their musings on love with psychology or biology. These studies form an interesting perspective on one of the most mysterious forces that shapes our world. However, as we move forward, we will concern ourselves with examining agape through an altogether different lens: ethics.

References

Armstrong, Arthur Hilary. 1961. "Platonic Eros and Christian *Agape*." The Downside Review 79 (255): 105-121. https://doi.org/10.1177/001258066107925502

Costello, Gwen. 2008. Spiritual Gems from Mother Teresa. Mystic: Twenty-Third Publications.

Giffords. 2022. "A Devastating Toll: 2021 CDC Data Shows Record Number of Gun Deaths, Makes Clear the Need for Continued Action to Address Gun Violence in America." Last modified July 14, 2022. https://giffords.org/press-release/2022/07/2021-cdc-data-shows- record-number-of-gun-deaths/

King Jr., Martin Luther. 1964. Strength to Love. New York: Pocket Books Inc.

Lamb, Christina, and Malala Yousafzai. 2013. I Am Malala: The Girl Who Stood Up for Education and Was Shot by the Taliban. New York: Little, Brown & Company.

Outka, Gene. 1977. *Agape*: An Ethical Analysis. New Haven: Yale University Press.

Secomb, Linnell. 2007. "Levinas: Love, Justice and Responsibility." In Philosophy and Love: From Plato to Popular Culture. 58-74. Edinburgh: Edinburgh University Press.

The Good Times. 2017. "Redemption: There Is Life After Hate." Last modified September 29, 2017. https://www.the-good-times.org/global-good/redemption-there-is-life-after-hate/

Wadell, Paul J. 2009. The Primacy of Love: An Introduction to the Ethics of Thomas Aquinas. Eugene: Wipf and Stock Publishers.

Xiaobo, Liu. 2012. "Using Truth to Undermine a System Built on Lies." Translated by Eva S. Chou. In No Enemies, No Hatred, 292-300. Cambridge: Harvard University Press.

About the Author

KC Love was born and raised in Detroit, Michigan. KC's love of family and friends is what's most important to her. When she is not spending time with her loved ones, you can find her writing, watching movies, or eating at one of her favorite restaurants. *Agape LOVE: Let Our Virtue Emerge* is KC's first book. KC believes love never fails.

Stay updated about new books and connect with KC here:

www.kconlove.com
facebook.com/KC Love
instagram.com/kconlove

www.ingramcontent.com/pod-product-compliance
Lightning Source LLC
Chambersburg PA
CBHW072137070526
44585CB00016B/1720